A Treatise on the Predestination of the Saints

A Treatise on the Predestination of the Saints

St. Augustine

A Treatise on the Predestination of the Saints

Written by: St. Augustine (Nov.13 354 – Aug.28 430)
Translated by Peter Holmes and Robert Ernest Wallis
Revised by: Professor Benjamin B. Warfield, D.D
Updated into Modern U.S English by A.M. Overett (b. 1960)

Published by
Lighthouse Christian Publishing
SAN 257-4330
5531 Dufferin Drive
Savage, Minnesota, 55378
United States of America

www.lighthousechristianpublishing.com

A TREATISE ON THE PREDESTINATION OF THE SAINTS,

BY AURELIUS AUGUSTIN, BISHOP OF HIPPO;

The First Book addressed to Prosper and Hilary. A.D. 428 or 429

Wherein the truth of predestination and grace is defended against the semi-Pelagians, —those people to wit, who by no means withdraw altogether from the Pelagian heresy, in that they contend that the beginning of salvation and of faith is of ourselves; so that in virtue, as it were, of this precedent merit, the other good gifts of God are attained. Augustin shows that not only the increase, but the very beginning also of faith is in God's gift. On this matter he does not disavow that he once thought differently, and that in some small works, written before his episcopate, he was in error, as in that exposition, which they object to him, of propositions from the epistle to the Romans. But he points out that he was subsequently convinced chiefly by this testimony, "but what hast thou that thou hast not received?" which he proves is to be taken as a testimony concerning faith itself also. He says that faith is to be counted among other works, which the apostle denies anticipating God's grace when He says, "not of works." He declares that the hardness of the heart is taken away by grace, and that all come to Christ who are taught to come by the Father; but that those whom He teaches, He teaches in mercy, while those whom He teaches not, in judgment He teaches not. That the passage from his hundred and second epistle, Question 2, "concerning the time of the Christian religion" which is alleged by the semi-Pelagians, may rightly be explained without detriment to the doctrine of grace and predestination. He teaches what is the difference between grace and predestination. Further, he says that God in his predestination foreknew what he had purposed to do. He marvels greatly that the adversaries of predestination, who are said to be unwilling to be dependent on the uncertainty of God's will, prefer rather to trust themselves to their own weakness than to the strength of God's promise. He clearly points out that they abuse this authority, "If thou believe, thou shalt be saved." That the truth of grace and perseverance shines forth in the case of infants that are saved, who are distinguished by no merits of their own from others who perish. For that there is no difference between them arising from the foreknowledge of merits which they would have had if they had lived longer. That testimony is wrongfully rejected by the adversaries as being uncanonical, which he adduced for the purpose of this discussion, "he was taken away lest wickedness," etc. That the most illustrious instance of predestination and grace is the Savior Himself, in whom a man obtained the privilege of being the Savior and the Only-begotten Son of God, through being assumed into oneness of person by the Word co-eternal with the Father, because of no precedent merits, either of works or of faith. That the predestinated are called by some certain calling peculiar to the elect, and that they have been elected before the foundation of the world; not because they were foreknown as men who would believe and would be holy, but in order that by means of that very election of grace they might be such, etc.

Chapter 1 [I.]—Introduction.

We know that in the Epistle to the Philippians the apostle said, "To write the same things to you to me indeed is not grievous but for you it is safe;" yet the same apostle writing to the Galatians when he saw that he had done enough among them of what he regarded as being needful for them, by the ministry of his preaching, said, "For the rest let no man cause me labor," or as it is read in many codices, "Let no one be troublesome to me." But although I confess that it causes me trouble that the divine word in which the grace of God is preached (which is absolutely no grace if it is given according to our merits), great and manifest as it is, is not yielded to, nevertheless my dearest sons, Prosper and Hilary, your zeal and brotherly affection—which makes you so reluctant to see any of the brethren in error, as to wish that, after so many books and letters of mine on this subject, I should write again from here—I love more than I can tell, although I do not dare to say that I love it as much as I ought. Wherefore, behold, I write to you again. And although not with you, yet through you I am still doing what I thought I had done sufficiently.

Chapter 2. —To What Extent the Massilians Withdraw from the Pelagians.

For on consideration of your letters, I seem to see that those brethren on whose behalf you exhibit a pious care that they may not hold the poetical opinion in which it is affirmed, "Everyone is a hope for himself," and so fall under that condemnation which is, not poetically, but prophetically, declared, "Cursed is every man that hath hope in man," must be treated in that way wherein the apostle dealt with those to whom he said, "And if in anything ye be otherwise minded, God shall reveal even this unto you." For as yet they are in darkness on the question concerning the predestination of the saints, but they have that whence, "if in anything they are otherwise minded, God will reveal even this unto them," if they are walking in that to which they have attained. For which reason the apostle, when he had said, "If ye are in anything otherwise minded, God shall reveal even this unto you," says, "Nevertheless whereunto we have attained, let us walk in the same." And those brethren of ours, on whose behalf your pious love is solicitous, have attained with Christ's Church to the belief that the human race is born obnoxious to the sin of the first man, and that none can be delivered from that evil save by the righteousness of the Second Man. Moreover, they have attained to the confession that men's wills are anticipated by God's grace; and to the agreement that no one can suffice to himself either for beginning or for completing any good work. These things, therefore, unto which they have attained, being held fast, abundantly distinguish them from the error of the Pelagians. Further, if they walk in them, and beseech Him who giveth understanding, if in anything concerning predestination they are otherwise minded, He will reveal even this unto them. Yet let us also spend upon them the influence of our love, and the ministry of our discourse, according to His gift, whom we have asked that in these letters we might say what should be suitable and profitable to them. For whence do we know whether by this our service, wherein we are serving them in the free love of Christ, our God may not perchance will to affect that purpose?

Chapter 3 [II.]—Even the Beginning of Faith is of God's Gift.

Therefore, I ought first to show that the faith by which we are Christians is the gift of God, if I can do that more thoroughly than I have already done in so many and so large volumes. But I see that I must now reply to those who say that the divine testimonies which I have adduced concerning this matter are of avail for this purpose, to assure us that we have faith itself of ourselves, but that its increase is of God; as if faith were not given to us by Him, but were only increased in us by Him, on the ground of the merit of its having begun from us. Thus there is here no departure from that opinion which Pelagius himself was constrained to condemn in the judgment of the bishops of Palestine, as is testified in the same Proceedings, "That the grace of God is given according to our merits," if it is not of God's grace that we begin to believe, but rather that on account of this beginning an addition is made to us of a more full and perfect belief; and so we first give the beginning of our faith to God, that His supplement may also be given to us again, and whatever else we faithfully ask.

Chapter 4. —Continuation of the Preceding.

But why do we not in opposition to this, rather hear the words, "Who hath first given to Him and it shall be recompensed to him again? since of Him, and through Him, and in Him, are all things." And from whom, then, is that very beginning of our faith if not from Him? For this is not excepted when other things are spoken of as of Him; but "of Him, and through Him, and in Him, are all things." But who can say that he who has already begun to believe deserves nothing from Him in whom he has believed? Whence it results that, to him who already deserves, other things are said to be added by a divine retribution, and thus that God's grace is given according to our merits. And this assertion when put before him, Pelagius himself condemned, that he might not be condemned. Whoever, then, wishes on every side to avoid this condemnable opinion, let him understand that what the apostle says is said with entire truthfulness, "Unto you it is given in the behalf of Christ not only to believe on Him, but also to suffer for His sake." He shows that both are the gifts of God, because he said that both were given. And he does not say, "to believe on Him more fully and perfectly," but, "to believe on Him." Neither does he say that he himself had obtained mercy to be more faithful, but "to be faithful," because he knew that he had not first given the beginning of his faith to God, and had its increase given back to him again by Him; but that he had been made faithful by God, who also had made him an apostle. For the beginnings of his faith are recorded, and they are very well known by being read in the church on an occasion calculated to distinguish them: how, being turned away from the faith which he was destroying, and being vehemently opposed to it, he was suddenly by a more powerful grace converted to it, by the conversion of Him, to whom as One who would do this very thing it was said by the prophet, "Thou wilt turn and quicken us;" so that not only from one who refused to believe he was made a willing believer, but, moreover, from being a persecutor, he suffered persecution in defense of that faith which he persecuted. Because it was given him by Christ "not only to believe on Him, but also to suffer for His sake."

Chapter 5. —To Believe is to Think with Assent.

And, therefore, commending that grace which is not given according to any merits, but is the cause of all good merits, he says, "Not that we are sufficient to think anything as of ourselves, but our sufficiency is of God." Let them give attention to this, and well weigh these words, who think that the beginning of faith is of ourselves, and the supplement of faith is of God. For who cannot see that thinking is prior to believing? For no one believes anything unless he has first thought that it is to be believed. For however suddenly, however rapidly, some thoughts fly before the will to believe, and this presently follows in such wise as to attend them, as it were, in closest conjunction, it is yet necessary that everything which is believed should be believed after thought has preceded; although even belief itself is nothing else than to think with assent. For it is not everyone who thinks that believes, since many think in order that they may not believe; but everybody who believes, thinks, —both thinks in believing and believes in thinking. Therefore, in what pertains to religion and piety (of which the apostle was speaking), if we are not capable of thinking anything as of ourselves, but our sufficiency is of God, we are certainly not capable of believing anything as of ourselves, since we cannot do this without thinking; but our sufficiency, by which we begin to believe, is of God. Wherefore, as no one is sufficient for himself, for the beginning or the completion of any good work whatever, —and this those brethren of yours, as what you have written intimates, already agree to be true, whence, as well in the beginning as in the carrying out of every good work, our sufficiency is of God, —so no one is sufficient for himself, either to begin or to perfect faith; but our sufficiency is of God. Because if faith is not a matter of thought, it is of no account; and we are not sufficient to think anything as of ourselves, but our sufficiency is of God.

Chapter 6. —Presumption and Arrogance to Be Avoided.

Care must be taken, brethren, beloved of God, that a man do not lift himself up in opposition to God, when he says that he does what God has promised. Was not the faith of the nations promised to Abraham, "and he, giving glory to God, most fully believed that what He promised He is able also to perform"? He therefore makes the faith of the nations, who can do what He has promised. Further, if God works our faith, acting in a wonderful manner in our hearts so that we believe, is there any reason to fear that He cannot do the whole; and does man on that account arrogate to himself its first elements, that he may merit to receive its last from God? Consider if in such a way any other result be gained than that the grace of God is given in some way or other, according to our merit, and so grace is no more grace. For on this principle it is rendered as debt, it is not given gratuitously; for it is due to the believer that his faith itself should be increased by the Lord, and that the increased faith should be the wages of the faith begun; nor is it observed when this is said, that this wage is assigned to believers, not of grace, but of debt. And I do not at all see why the whole should not be attributed to man,—as he who could originate for himself what he had not previously, can himself increase what he had originated,—except that it is impossible to withstand the most manifest divine testimony by which faith, whence piety takes its beginning, is shown also to be the gift of God: such as is that testimony that "God hath dealt to every man the measure of faith;" and that one, "Peace be to the brethren, and love with faith, from God the Father, and the Lord Jesus Christ," and other similar passages. Man, therefore, unwilling to resist such clear testimonies as these, and yet desiring himself to have the merit of believing, compounds as it were with God to claim a portion of faith for himself, and to leave a portion for Him; and, what is still more arrogant, he takes the first portion for himself and gives the subsequent to Him; and so in that which he says belongs to both, he makes himself the first, and God the second!

Chapter 7 [III.]—Augustin Confesses that He Had Formerly Been in Error Concerning the Grace of God.

It was not thus that that pious and humble teacher thought—I speak of the most blessed Cyprian—when he said, "that we must boast in nothing, since nothing is our own." And in order to show this, he appealed to the apostle as a witness, where he said, "For what hast thou that thou hast not received? And if thou hast received it, why boasts thou as if thou have not received it?" And it was chiefly by this testimony that I myself also was convinced when I was in a similar error, thinking that faith whereby we believe on God is not God's gift, but that it is in us from ourselves, and that by it we obtain the gifts of God, whereby we may live temperately and righteously and piously in this world. For I did not think that faith was preceded by God's grace, so that by its means would be given to us what we might profitably ask, except that we could not believe if the proclamation of the truth did not precede; but that we should consent when the gospel was preached to us I thought was our own doing, and came to us from ourselves. And this my error is sufficiently indicated in some small works of mine written before my episcopate. Among these is that which you have mentioned in your letters wherein is an exposition of certain propositions from the Epistle to the Romans. Eventually, when I was retracting all my small works, and was committing that retractation to writing, of which task I had already completed two books before I had taken up your more lengthy letters,—when in the first volume I had reached the retractation of this book, I then spoke thus:—"Also discussing, I say, 'what God could have chosen in him who was as yet unborn, whom He said that the elder should serve; and what in the same elder, equally as yet unborn, He could have rejected; concerning whom, on this account, the prophetic testimony is recorded, although declared long subsequently, "Jacob have I loved, and Esau have I hated,"' I carried out my reasoning to the point of saying: 'God did not therefore choose the works of any one in foreknowledge of what He Himself would give them, but he chose the faith, in the foreknowledge that He would choose that very person whom He foreknew would believe on Him,—to whom He would give the Holy Spirit, so that by doing good works he might obtain eternal life also.' I had not yet very carefully sought, nor had I as yet found, what is the nature of the election of grace, of which the apostle says, 'A remnant are saved according to the election of grace.' Which assuredly is not grace if any merits precede it; lest what is now given, not according to grace, but according to debt, be rather paid to merits than freely given. And what I next subjoined: 'For the same apostle says, "The same God which worketh all in all;" but it was never said, God believeth all in all;' and then added, 'Therefore what we believe is our own, but what good thing we do is of Him who giveth the Holy Spirit to them that believe:' I certainly could not have said, had I already known that faith itself also is found among those gifts of God which are given by the same Spirit. Both, therefore, are ours because of the choice of the will, and yet both are given by the spirit of faith and love. For faith is not alone but as it is written, 'Love with faith, from God the Father, and our Lord Jesus Christ.' And what I said a little after, 'For it is ours to believe and to will, but it is His to give to those who believe and will, the power of doing good works through the Holy Spirit, by whom love is shed abroad in our hearts,'—is true indeed; but by the same rule both are also God's, because God prepares the will; and both are ours too, because they are only brought about with our good wills. And thus what I subsequently said also: 'Because we are not able to will unless we are called; and when, after our calling, we would will, our willing is not sufficiently nor our running, unless God gives strength to us that run, and leads us whither He calls us;' and thereupon added: 'It is plain, therefore, that it is not of him that wills, nor of him that runs, but of God that shows mercy, that we do good works'—this is absolutely most true. But I discovered little concerning the calling itself, which is according to God's purpose; for not such is the calling of all that are called, but only of the elect. Therefore, what I said a little afterwards: 'For as in those whom God elects it is not works but faith that begins the merit so as to do good works by the gift of God, so in those whom He condemns, unbelief and impiety begin the merit of punishment, so that even by way of punishment itself they do evil works'—I spoke most truly. But that even the merit itself of faith was God's gift, I neither thought of inquiring into, nor did I say. And in another place, I say: 'For whom He has mercy upon, He makes to do good works, and whom He hardened He leaves to do evil works; but that mercy is bestowed upon the preceding merit of faith, and that hardening is applied to preceding iniquity.' And this indeed is true; but it should further have been asked, whether even the merit of faith does not come from God's mercy, —that is, whether that mercy is manifested in man only because he is a believer, or whether it is also manifested that he may be a believer? For we read in the apostle's words: 'I obtained mercy to be a believer.' He does not say, 'Because I was a believer.' Therefore, although it is given to the believer, yet it has been given also that he may be a believer. Therefore also, in another place in the same book I most truly said: 'Because, if it is of God's mercy, and not of works, that we are even called that we may believe, and it is granted to us who believe to do good works, that mercy must not be grudged to the heathen;'—although I there discoursed less carefully about that calling which is given according to God's purpose."

Chapter 8 [IV.]—What Augustin Wrote to Simplicianus, the Successor of Ambrose, Bishop of Milan.

You see plainly what was at that time my opinion concerning faith and works, although I was laboring in commending God's grace; and in this opinion I see that those brethren of ours now are, because they have not been as careful to make progress with me in my writings as they were in reading them. For if they had been so careful, they would have found that question solved in accordance with the truth of the divine Scriptures in the first book of the two which I wrote in the very beginning of my episcopate to Simplicianus, of blessed memory, Bishop of the Church of Milan, and successor to St. Ambrose. Unless, perchance, they may not have known these books; in which case, take care that they do know them. Of this first of those two books, I first spoke in the second book of the Retractations; and what I said is as follows: "Of the books, I say, on which, as a bishop, I have labored, the first two are addressed to Simplicianus, president of the Church of Milan, who succeeded the most blessed Ambrose, concerning divers questions, two of which I gathered into the first book from the Epistle of Paul the Apostle to the Romans. The former of them is about what is written: 'What shall we say, then? Is the law sin? By no means;' as far as the passage where he says, 'Who shall deliver me from the body of this death? The grace of God through Jesus Christ our Lord.' And therein I have expounded those words of the apostle: 'The law is spiritual; but I am carnal,' and others in which the flesh is declared to be in conflict against the Spirit in such a way as if a man were there described as still under law, and not yet established under grace. For, long afterwards, I perceived that those words might even be (and probably were) the utterance of a spiritual man. The latter question in this book is gathered from that passage where the apostle says, 'And not only this, but when Rebecca also had conceived by one act of intercourse, even by our father Isaac,' as far as that place where he says, 'Except the Lord of Sabaoth had left us a seed, we should be as Sodom, and should have been like unto Gomorrah.' In the solution of this question I labored indeed on behalf of the free choice of the human will, but God's grace overcame, and I could only reach that point where the apostle is perceived to have said with the most evident truth, 'For who makes thee to differ? and what hast thou that thou hast not received? Now, if thou hast received it, why dost thou glory as if thou receive it not?' And this the martyr Cyprian was also desirous of setting forth when he compressed the whole of it in that title: 'That we must boast in nothing, since nothing is our own.'" This is why I previously said that it was chiefly by this apostolic testimony that I myself had been convinced, when I thought otherwise concerning this matter; and this God revealed to me as I sought to solve this question when I was writing, as I said, to the Bishop Simplicianus. This testimony, therefore, of the apostle, when for the sake of repressing man's conceit he said, "For what hast thou which thou hast not received?" does not allow any believer to say, I have faith which I received not. All the arrogance of this answer is absolutely repressed by these apostolic words. Moreover, it cannot even be said, "Although I have not a perfected faith, yet I have its beginning, whereby I first of all believed in Christ." Because here also is answered: "But what hast thou that thou hast not received? Now, if thou hast received it, why dost thou glory as if thou receive it not?"

Chapter 9 [V.]—The Purpose of the Apostle in

These Words.

The notion, however, which they entertain, "that these words, 'What hast thou that thou hast not received?' cannot be said of this faith, because it has remained in the same nature, although corrupted, which at first was endowed with health and perfection," is perceived to have no force for the purpose that they desire if it be considered why the apostle said these words. For he was concerned that no one should glory in man, because dissensions had sprung up among the Corinthian Christians, so that everyone was saying, "I, indeed, am of Paul, and another, I am of Apollos, and another, I am of Cephas;" and thence he went on to say: "God hath chosen the foolish things of the world to confound the wise; and God hath chosen the weak things of the world to confound the strong things; and God hath chosen the ignoble things of the world, and contemptible things, and those things which are not, to make of no account things which are; that no flesh should glory before God." Here the intention of the apostle is of a certainty sufficiently plain against the pride of man, that no one should glory in man; and thus, no one should glory in himself. Finally, when he had said "that no flesh should glory before God," in order to show in what man ought to glory, he immediately added, "But it is of Him that ye are in Christ Jesus, who is made unto us wisdom from God, and righteousness, and sanctification, and redemption: that according as it is written, He that glories, let him glory in the Lord." Thence that intention of his progressed, till afterwards rebuking them he says, "For ye are yet carnal; for whereas there are among you envying and contention, are ye not carnal, and walk according to man? For while one saith I am of Paul, and another, I am of Apollos, are ye not men? What, then, is Apollos, and what Paul? Ministers by whom you believed; and to everyone as the Lord has given. I have planted, and Apollos watered; but God gave the increase. Therefore, neither is he that planted anything, nor he that watered, but God that giveth the increase." Do you not see that the sole purpose of the apostle is that man may be humbled, and God alone exalted? Since in all those things, indeed, which are planted and watered, he says that not even are the planter and the waterer anything, but God who giveth the increase: and the very fact, also, that one plants and another waters he attributes not to themselves, but to God, when he says, "To everyone as the Lord hath given; I have planted, Apollos watered." Hence, therefore, persisting in the same intention he comes to the point of saying, "Therefore let no man glory in man," for he had already said, "He that glories, let him glory in the Lord." After these and some other matters which are associated therewith, that same intention of his is carried on in the words: "And these things, brethren, I have in a figure transferred to myself and to Apollos for your sakes, that ye might learn in us that no one of you should be puffed up for one against another above that which is written. For who makes thee to differ? And what hast thou which thou hast not received? Now, if thou hast received it, why dost thou glory as if thou receive it not?"

Chapter 10. —It is God's Grace Which Specially Distinguishes One Man from Another.

In this the apostle's most evident intention, in which he speaks against human pride, so that none should glory in man but in God, it is too absurd, as I think, to suppose God's natural gifts, whether man's entire and perfected nature itself as it was bestowed on him in his first state, or the remains, whatever they may be, of his degraded nature. For is it by such gifts as these, which are common to all men, that men are distinguished from men? But here he first said, "For who makes thee to differ?" and then added, "And what hast thou that thou hast not received?" Because a man, puffed up against another, might say, "My faith makes me to differ," or "My righteousness," or anything else of the kind. In reply to such notions, the good teacher says, "But what hast thou that thou hast not received?" And from whom but from Him who makes thee to differ from another, on whom He bestowed not what He bestowed on thee? "Now if," says he, "thou hast received it, why dost thou glory as if thou receive it not?" Is he concerned, I ask, about anything else save that he who glories should glory in the Lord? But nothing is so opposed to this feeling as for anyone to glory concerning his own merits in such a way as if he himself had made them for himself, and not the grace of God, —a grace, however, which makes the good to differ from the wicked, and is not common to the good and the wicked. Let the grace, therefore, whereby we are living and reasonable creatures, and are distinguished from cattle, be attributed to nature; let that grace also by which, among men themselves, the handsome are made to differ from the ill-formed, or the intelligent from the stupid, or anything of that kind, be ascribed to nature. But he whom the apostle was rebuking did not puff himself up as contrasted with cattle, nor as contrasted with any other man, in respect of any natural endowment which might be found even in the worst of men. But he ascribed to himself, and not to God, some good gift which pertained to a holy life, and was puffed up therewith when he deserved to hear the rebuke, "Who hath made thee to differ? and what hast thou that thou receive not?" For though the capacity to have faith is of nature, is it also of nature to have it? "For all men have not faith," although all men have the capacity to have faith. But the apostle does not say, "And what hast thou capacity to have, the capacity to have which thou receive not?" but he says, "And what hast thou which thou receive not?" Accordingly, the capacity to have faith, as the capacity to have love, belongs to men's nature; but to have faith, even as to have love, belongs to the grace of believers. That nature, therefore, in which is given to us the capacity of having faith, does not distinguish man from man, but faith itself makes the believer to differ from the unbeliever. And thus, when it is said, "For who makes thee to differ? and what hast thou that thou receives not?" if any one dare to say, "I have faith of myself, I did not, therefore, receive it," he directly contradicts this most manifest truth,—not because it is not in the choice of man's will to believe or not to believe, but because in the elect the will is prepared by the Lord. Thus, moreover, the passage, "For who makes thee to differ? and what hast thou that thou receive not?" refers to that very faith which is in the will of man.

Chapter 11 [VI.]—That Some Men are Elected is of God's Mercy.

"Many hear the word of truth; but some believe, while others contradict. Therefore, the former will to believe; the latter do not will." Who does not know this?

Who can deny this? But since in some the will is prepared by the Lord, in others it is not prepared, we must assuredly be able to distinguish what comes from God's mercy, and what from His judgment. "What Israel sought for," says the apostle, "he hath not obtained, but the election hath obtained it; and the rest were blinded, as it is written, God gave to them the spirit of compunction, — eyes that they should not see, and ears that they should not hear, even to this day. And David said, Let their table be made a snare, a retribution, and a stumbling block to them; let their eyes be darkened, that they may not see; and bow down their back always." Here is mercy and judgment, —mercy towards the election which has obtained the righteousness of God, but judgment to the rest which have been blinded. And yet the former, because they willed, believed; the latter, because they did not will believed not. Therefore, mercy and judgment were manifested in the very wills themselves. Certainly, such an election is of grace, not at all of merits. For he had before said, "So, therefore, even at this present time, the remnant has been saved by the election of grace. And if by grace, now it is no more of works; otherwise grace is no more grace." Therefore, the election obtained what it obtained gratuitously; there preceded none of those things which they might first give, and it should be given to them again. He saved them for nothing. But to the rest who were blinded, as is there plainly declared, it was done in recompense. "All the paths of the Lord are mercy and truth." But His ways are unsearchable. Therefore, the mercy by which He freely delivers, and the truth by which He righteously judges, are equally unsearchable.

Chapter 12 [VII.]—Why the Apostle Said that We are Justified by Faith and Not by Works.

But perhaps it may be said: "The apostle distinguishes faith from works; he says, indeed, that grace is not of works, but he does not say that it is not of faith." This, indeed, is true. But Jesus says that faith itself also is the work of God, and commands us to work it. For the Jews said to Him, "What shall we do that we may work the work of God? Jesus answered, and said unto them, This is the work of God, that ye believe on Him whom He hath sent." The apostle, therefore, distinguishes faith from works, just as Judah is distinguished from Israel in the two kingdoms of the Hebrews, although Judah is Israel itself. And he says that a man is justified by faith and not by works, because faith itself is first given, from which may be obtained other things which are specially characterized as works, in which a man may live righteously. For he himself also says, "By grace ye are saved through faith; and this not of yourselves; but it is the gift of God,"—that is to say, "And in saying 'through faith,' even faith itself is not of yourselves, but is God's gift." "Not of works," he says, "lest any man should be lifted up." For it is often said, "He deserved to believe, because he was a good man even before he believed." Which may be said of Cornelius since his alms were accepted and his prayers heard before he had believed on Christ; and yet without some faith he neither gave alms nor prayed. For how did he call on him on whom he had not believed? But if he could have been saved without the faith of Christ the Apostle Peter would not have been sent as an architect to build him up; although, "Except the Lord build the house, they labor in vain who build it."

And we are told, Faith is of ourselves; other things which pertain to works of righteousness are of the Lord; as if faith did not belong to the building, —as if, I say, the foundation did not belong to the building. But if this primarily and especially belongs to it, he labors in vain who seeks to build up the faith by preaching, unless the Lord in His mercy builds it up from within. Whatever, therefore, of good works Cornelius performed, as well before he believed in Christ as when he believed and after he had believed, are all to be ascribed to God, lest, perchance any man be lifted up.

Chapter 13 [VIII.]—The Effect of Divine Grace.

Accordingly, our only Master and Lord Himself, when He had said what I have above mentioned, — "This is the work of God, that ye believe on Him whom He hath sent,"—says a little afterwards in that same discourse of His, "I said unto you that ye also have seen me and have not believed. All that the Father giveth me shall come to me." What is the meaning of "shall come to me," but, "shall believe in me"? But it is the Father's gift that this may be the case. Moreover, a little after He says, "Murmur not among yourselves. No one can come to me, except the Father which hath sent me draw him; and I will raise him up at the last day. It is written in the prophets, And they shall be all teachable of God. Every man that hath heard of the Father, and hath learned, cometh unto me." What is the meaning of, "Every man that hath heard from the Father, and hath learned, cometh unto me," except that there is none who hears from the Father, and learns, who cometh not to me? For if everyone who has heard from the Father, and has learned, comes, certainly everyone who does not come has not heard from the Father; for if he had heard and learned, he would come. For no one has heard and learned, and has not come; but everyone, as the Truth declares, who has heard from the Father, and has learned, comes. Far removed from the senses of the flesh is this teaching in which the Father is heard and teaches to come to the Son. Engaged herein is also the Son Himself, because He is His Word by which He thus teaches; and He does not do this through the ear of the flesh, but of the heart. Herein engaged, also, at the same time, is the Spirit of the Father and of the Son; and He, too, teaches, and does not teach separately, since we have learned that the workings of the Trinity are inseparable. And that is certainly the same Holy Spirit of whom the apostle says, "We, however, having the same Spirit of faith." But this is especially attributed to the Father, because of Him is begotten the Only Begotten, and from Him proceeds the Holy Spirit, of which it would be tedious to argue more elaborately; and I think that my work in fifteen books on the Trinity which God is, has already reached you. Very far removed, I say, from the senses of the flesh is this instruction wherein God is heard and teaches. We see that many come to the Son because we see that many believe on Christ, but when and how they have heard this from the Father, and have learned, we see not. It is true that that grace is exceedingly secret, but who doubts that it is grace? This grace, therefore, which is hiddenly bestowed in human hearts by the Divine gift, is rejected by no hard heart, because it is given for the sake of first taking away the hardness of the heart. When, therefore, the Father is heard within, and teaches, so that a man comes to the Son, He takes away the heart of stone and gives a heart of flesh, as in the declaration of the prophet He has promised. Because He thus makes them children and vessels of mercy which He has prepared for glory.

Chapter 14. —Why the Father Does Not Teach All that They May Come to Christ.

Why, then, does He not teach all that they may come to Christ, except because all whom He teaches, He teaches in mercy, while those whom He teaches not, in judgment He teaches not? Since, "On whom He will He has mercy, and whom He will He hardened." But He has mercy when He gives good things. He hardens when He recompenses what is deserved. Or if, as some would prefer to distinguish them, those words also are his to whom the apostle says, "Thou says then unto me," so that he may be regarded as having said, "Therefore hath He mercy on whom He will, and whom He will He hardened," as well as those which follow,—to wit, "What is it that is still complained of? for who resists His will?" does the apostle answer, "O man, what thou hast said is false?" No; but he says, "O man, who art thou that replies against God? Doth the thing formed say to him that formed it, Why hast thou made me thus? Hath not the potter power over the clay of the same lump?" and what follows, which you very well know. And yet in a certain sense the Father teaches all men to come to His Son. For it was not in vain that it was written in the prophets, "And they shall all be teachable of God." And when He too had premised this testimony, He added, "Every man, therefore, who has heard of the Father, and has learned, cometh to me." As, therefore, we speak justly when we say concerning any teacher of literature who is alone in a city, He teaches literature here to everybody, —not that all men learn, but that there is none who learns literature there who does not learn from him, —so we justly say, God teaches all men to come to Christ, not because all come, but because none comes in any other way. And why He does not teach all men the apostle explained, as far as he judged that it was to be explained, because, "willing to show His wrath, and to exhibit His power, He endured with much patience the vessels of wrath which were perfected for destruction; and that He might make known the riches of His glory on the vessels of mercy which He has prepared for glory." Hence it is that the "word of the cross is foolishness to them that perish; but unto them that are saved it is the power of God." God teaches all such to come to Christ, for He wills all such to be saved, and to come to the knowledge of the truth. And if He had willed to teach even those to whom the word of the cross is foolishness to come to Christ, beyond all doubt these also would have come. For He neither deceives nor is deceived when He says, "Everyone that hath heard of the Father, and hath learned, cometh to me." Away, then, with the thought that any one cometh not, who has heard of the Father and has learned.

Chapter 15. —It is Believers that are Taught of God.

"Why," say they, "does He not teach all men?" If we should say that they whom He does not teach are unwilling to learn, we shall be met with the answer: And what becomes of what is said to Him, "O God, Thou wilt turn us again, and quicken us"? Or if God does not make men willing who were not willing, on what principle does the Church pray, according to the Lord's commandment, for her persecutors? For thus also the blessed Cyprian would have it to be understood that we say, "Thy will be done, as in heaven so in earth,"—that is, as in those who have already believed, and who are, as it were, heaven, so also in those who do not believe, and on this account are still the earth. What, then, do we pray for on behalf of those who are unwilling to believe, except that God would work in them to will also? Certainly the apostle says, "Brethren, my heart's good will, indeed, and my prayer to God for them, is for their salvation." He prays for those who do not believe, —for what, except that they may believe? For in no other way do they obtain salvation. If, then, the faith of the petitioners precede the grace of God, does the faith of them on whose behalf prayer is made that they may believe precede the grace of God? —since this is the very thing that is besought for them, that on them that believe not—that is, who have not faith—faith itself may be bestowed? When, therefore, the gospel is preached, some believe, some believe not; but they who believe at the voice of the preacher from without, hear of the Father from within, and learn; while they who do not believe, hear outwardly, but inwardly do not hear nor learn; —that is to say, to the former it is given to believe; to the latter it is not given. Because "no man," says He, "cometh to me, except the Father which sent me draw him." And this is more plainly said afterwards. For after a little time, when He was speaking of eating his flesh and drinking His blood, and some even of His disciples said, "This is a hard saying, who can hear it? Jesus, knowing in Himself that His disciples murmured at this, said unto them, Doth this offend you?" And a little after He said, "The words that I have spoken unto you are spirit and life;

but there are some among you which believe not." And immediately the evangelist says, "For Jesus knew from the beginning who were the believers, and who should betray Him; and He said, Therefore said I unto you, that no man can come unto me except it were given him of my Father." Therefore, to be drawn to Christ by the Father, and to hear and learn of the Father in order to come to Christ, is nothing else than to receive from the Father the gift by which to believe in Christ. For it was not the hearers of the gospel that were distinguished from those who did not hear, but the believers from those who did not believe, by Him who said, "No man cometh to me except it were given him of my Father."

Chapter 16. —Why the Gift of Faith is Not Given to All.

Faith, then, as well in its beginning as in its completion, is God's gift; and let no one have any doubt whatever, unless he desires to resist the plainest sacred writings, that this gift is given to some, while to some it is not given. But why it is not given to all ought not to disturb the believer, who believes that from one all have gone into a condemnation, which undoubtedly is most righteous; so that even if none were delivered therefrom, there would be no just cause for finding fault with God. Whence it is plain that it is a great grace for many to be delivered, and to acknowledge in those that are not delivered what would be due to themselves; so that he that glories may glory not in his own merits, which he sees to be equaled in those that are condemned, but in the Lord. But why He delivers one rather than another, — "His judgments are unsearchable, and His ways past finding out." For it is better in this case for us to hear or to say, "O man, who art thou that replies against God?" than to dare to speak as if we could know what He has chosen to be kept secret. Since, moreover, He could not will anything unrighteous.

Chapter 17 [IX.]—His Argument in His Letter Against Porphyry, as to Why the Gospel Came So Late into the World.

But that which you remember my saying in a certain small treatise of mine against Porphyry, under the title of The Time of the Christian Religion, I so said for the sake of escaping this more careful and elaborate argument about grace; although its meaning, which could be unfolded elsewhere or by others, was not wholly omitted, although I had been unwilling in that place to explain it. For, among other matters, I spoke thus in answer to the question proposed, why it was after so long a time that Christ came: "Accordingly, I say, since they do not object to Christ that all do not follow His teaching (for even they themselves feel that this could not be objected at all with any justice, either to the wisdom of the philosophers or even to the deity of their own gods), what will they reply, if—leaving out of the question that depth of God's wisdom and knowledge where perchance some other divine plan is far more secretly hidden, without prejudging also other causes, which cannot be traced out by the wise—we say to them only this, for the sake of brevity in the arguing of this question, that Christ willed to appear to men, and that His doctrine should be preached among them, at that time when He knew, and at that place where He knew, that there were some who would believe on Him. For at those times, and in those places, at which His gospel was not preached, He foreknew that all would be in His preaching such as, not indeed all, but many were in His bodily presence, who would not believe on Him, even when the dead were raised by Him; such as we see many now, who, although the declarations of the prophets concerning Him are fulfilled by such manifestations, are still unwilling to believe, and prefer to resist by human astuteness, rather than yield to divine authority so clear and perspicuous, and so lofty, and sublimely made known, so long as the human understanding is small and weak in its approach to divine truth. What wonder is it, then, if Christ knew the world in former ages to be so full of unbelievers, that He should reasonably refuse to appear, or to be preached to them, who, as He foreknew, would believe neither His words nor His miracles? For it is not incredible that all at that time were such as from His coming even to the present time we marvel that so many have been and are. And yet from the beginning of the human race, sometimes more hiddenly, sometimes more evidently, even as to Divine Providence the times seemed to be fitting, there has neither been a failure of prophecy, nor were there wanting those who believed on Him; as well from Adam to Moses, as in the people of Israel itself which by a certain special mystery was a prophetic people; and in other nations before He had come in the flesh. For as some are mentioned in the sacred Hebrew books, as early as the time of Abraham, —neither of his fleshly race nor of the people of Israel nor of the foreign society among the people of Israel, —who were, nevertheless, sharers in their sacrament, why may we not believe that there were others elsewhere among other people, here and there, although we do not read any mention of them in the same authorities? Thus the salvation of this religion, by which only true one true salvation is truly promised, never failed him who was worthy of it; and whoever it failed was not worthy of it. And from the very beginning of the propagation of man, even to the end, the gospel is preached, to some for a reward, to some for judgment; and thus also those to whom the faith was not announced at all were foreknown as those who would not believe; and those to whom it was announced, although they were not such as would believe, are set forth as an example for the former; while those to whom it is announced who should believe, are prepared for the kingdom of heaven, and the company of the holy angels."

Chapter 18. —The Preceding Argument Applied to the Present Time.

Do you not see that my desire was, without any prejudgment of the hidden counsel of God, and of other reasons, to say what might seem sufficient about Christ's foreknowledge, to convince the unbelief of the pagans who had brought forward this question? For what is truer than that Christ foreknew who should believe on Him, and at what times and places they should believe? But whether by the preaching of Christ to themselves by themselves they were to have faith, or whether they would receive it by God's gift, —that is, whether God only foreknew them, or also predestinated them, I did not at that time think it necessary to inquire or to discuss. Therefore what I said, "that Christ willed to appear to men at that time, and that His doctrine should be preached among them when He knew, and where He knew, that there were those who would believe on Him," may also thus be said, "That Christ willed to appear to men at that time, and that His gospel should be preached among those, whom He knew, and where He knew, that there were those who had been elected in Himself before the foundation of the world." But since, if it were so said, it would make the reader desirous of asking about those things which now by the warning of Pelagian errors must of necessity be discussed with greater copiousness and care, it seemed to me that what at that time was sufficient should be briefly said, leaving to one side, as I said, the depth of the wisdom and knowledge of God, and without prejudging other reasons, concerning which I thought that we might more fittingly argue, not then, but at some other time.

Chapter 19 [X]—In What Respects Predestination and Grace Differ.

Moreover, that which I said, "That the salvation of this religion has never been lacking to him who was worthy of it, and that he to whom it was lacking was not worthy,"—if it be discussed and it be asked whence any man can be worthy, there are not wanting those who say—by human will. But we say, by divine grace or predestination. Further, between grace and predestination there is only this difference, that predestination is the preparation for grace, while grace is the donation itself. When, therefore the apostle says, "Not of works, lest any man should boast. For we are His workmanship, created in Christ Jesus in good works," it is grace; but what follows— "which God hath prepared that we should walk in them"—is predestination, which cannot exist without foreknowledge, although foreknowledge may exist without predestination; because God foreknew by predestination those things which He was about to do, whence it was said, "He made those things that shall be." Moreover, He is able to foreknow even those things which He does not Himself do, —as all sins whatever. Because, although there are some which are in such wise sins as that they are also the penalties of sins, whence it is said, "God gave them over to a reprobate mind, to do those things which are not convenient," it is not in such a case the sin that is God's, but the judgment. Therefore God's predestination of good is, as I have said, the preparation of grace; which grace is the effect of that predestination. Therefore, when God promised to Abraham in his seed the faith of the nations, saying, "I have established thee a father of many nations," whence the apostle says, "Therefore it is of faith, that the promise, according to grace, might be established to all the seed," He promised not from the power of our will but from His own predestination. For He promised what He Himself would do, not what men would do. Because, although men do those good things which pertain to God's worship, He Himself makes them to do what He has commanded; it is not they that cause Him to do what He has promised. Otherwise the fulfilment of God's promises would not be in the power of God, but in that of men; and thus what was promised by God to Abraham would be given to Abraham by men themselves. Abraham, however, did not believe thus, but "he believed, giving glory to God, that what He promised He is able also to do." He does not say, "to foretell"—he does not say, "to foreknow;" for He can foretell and foreknow the doings of strangers also; but he says, "He is able also to do;" and thus he is speaking not of the doings of others, but of His own.

Chapter 20. —Did God Promise the Good Works of the Nations and Not Their Faith, to Abraham?

Did God, perchance, promise to Abraham in his seed the good works of the nations, so as to promise that which He Himself does, but did not promise the faith of the Gentiles, which men do for themselves; but so as to promise what He Himself does, did He foreknow that men would affect that faith? The apostle, indeed, does not speak thus, because God promised children to Abraham, who should follow the footsteps of his faith, as he very plainly says. But if He promised the works, and not the faith of the Gentiles certainly since they are not good works unless they are of faith (for "the righteous lives of faith," and, "Whatsoever is not of faith is sin," and, "Without faith it is impossible to please"), it is nevertheless in man's power that God should fulfil what He has promised. For unless man should do what without the gift of God pertains to man, he will not cause God to give, —that is, unless man have faith of himself. God does not fulfil what He has promised, that works of righteousness should be given by God. And thus that God should be able to fulfil His promises is not in God's power, but man's. And if truth and piety do not forbid our believing this, let us believe with Abraham, that what He has promised He is able also to perform. But He promised children to Abraham; and this men cannot be unless they have faith, therefore He gives faith also.

Chapter 21. —It is to Be Wondered at that Men Should Rather Trust to Their Own Weakness Than to God's Strength.

Certainly, when the apostle says, "Therefore it is of faith that the promise may be sure according to grace," I marvel that men would rather entrust themselves to their own weakness, than to the strength of God's promise. But says thou, God's will concerning myself is to me uncertain? What then? Is thine own will concerning thyself certain to thee? and dost thou not fear, — "Let him that thinketh he stands take heed lest he fall"? Since, then, both are uncertain, why does not man commit his faith, hope, and love to the stronger will rather than to the weaker?

Chapter 22. —God's Promise is Sure.

"But," say they, "when it is said, 'If thou believe, thou shalt be saved,' one of these things is required; the other is offered. What is required is in man's power; what is offered is in God's." Why are not both in God's, as well what He commands as what He offers? For He is asked to give what He commands. Believers ask that their faith may be increased; they ask on behalf of those who do not believe, that faith may be given to them; therefore both in its increase and in its beginnings, faith is the gift of God. But it is said thus: "If thou believe, thou shalt be saved," in the same way that it is said, "If by the Spirit ye shall mortify the deeds of the flesh, ye shall live." For in this case also, of these two things one is required, the other is offered. It is said, "If by the Spirit ye shall mortify the deeds of the flesh, ye shall live." Therefore, that we mortify the deeds of the flesh is required, but that we may live is offered. Is it, then, fitting for us to say, that to mortify the deeds of the flesh is not a gift of God, and not to confess it to be a gift of God, because we hear it required of us, with the offer of life as a reward if we shall do it? Away with this being approved by the partakers and champions of grace! This is the condemnable error of the Pelagians, whose mouths the apostle immediately stopped when he added, "For as many as are led by the Spirit of God, they are the sons of God;" lest we should believe that we mortify the deeds of the flesh, not by God's Spirit, but by our own. And of this Spirit of God, moreover, he was speaking in that place where he says, "But all these worketh that one and the self-same Spirit, dividing unto every man what is his own, as He will;" and among all these things, as you know, he also named faith. As, therefore, although it is the gift of God to mortify the deeds of the flesh, yet it is required of us, and life is set before us as a reward; so also faith is the gift of God, although when it is said, "If thou believe, thou shalt be saved," faith is required of us, and salvation is proposed to us as a reward. For these things are both commanded us, and are shown to be God's gifts, in order that we may understand both that we do them, and that God makes us to do them, as He most plainly says by the prophet Ezekiel. For what is plainer than when He says, "I will cause you to do"? Give heed to that passage of Scripture, and you will see that God promises that He will make them to do those things which He commands to be done. He truly is not silent as to the merits but as to the evil deeds, of those to whom He shows that He is returning good for evil, by the very fact that He causes them thenceforth to have good works, in causing them to do the divine commands.

Chapter 23 [XII.]—Remarkable Illustrations of Grace and Predestination in Infants, and in Christ.

But all this reasoning, whereby we maintain that the grace of God through Jesus Christ our Lord is truly grace, that is, is not given according to our merits, although it is most manifestly asserted by the witness of the divine declarations, yet, among those who think that they are withheld from all zeal for piety unless they can attribute to themselves something, which they first give that it may be recompensed to them again, involves somewhat of a difficulty in respect of the condition of grown-up people, who are already exercising the choice of will. But when we come to the case of infants, and to the Mediator between God and man Himself, the man Christ Jesus, there is wanting all assertion of human merits that precede the grace of God, because the former are not distinguished from others by any preceding good merits that they should belong to the Deliverer of men; any more than He Himself being Himself a man, was made the Deliverer of men by virtue of any precedent human merits.

Chapter 24. —That No One is Judged According to What He Would Have Done If He Had Lived Longer.

For who can hear that infants, baptized in the condition of mere infancy, are said to depart from this life by reason of their future merits, and that others not baptized are said to die in the same age because their future merits are foreknown, —but as evil; so that God rewards or condemns in them not their good or evil life, but no life at all? The apostle, indeed, fixed a limit which man's incautious suspicion, to speak gently, ought not to transgress, for he says, "We shall all stand before the judgment-seat of Christ; that everyone may receive according to the things which he has done by means of the body, whether it be good or evil." "Has done," he said; and he did not add, "or would have done." But I know not whence this thought should have entered the minds of such men, that infants' future merits (which shall not be) should be punished or honored. But why is it said that a man is to be judged according to those things which he has done by means of the body, when many things are done by the mind alone, and not by the body, nor by any member of the body; and for the most part things of such importance, that a most righteous punishment would be due to such thought, such as,—to say nothing of others,—that "The fool hath said in his heart there is no God"? What, then, is the meaning of, "According to those things that he hath done by means of the body," except according to those things which he has done during that time in which he was in the body, so that we may understand "by means of the body" as meaning "throughout the season of bodily life"? But after the body, no one will be in the body except at the last resurrection, —not for the purpose of establishing any claims of merit, but for the sake of receiving recompenses for good merits, and enduring punishments for evil merits. But in this intermediate period between the putting off and the taking again of the body, the souls are either tormented or they are in repose, according to those things which they have done during the period of the bodily life. And to this period of the bodily life moreover pertains, what the

Pelagians deny, but Christ's Church confesses, original sin; and according to whether this is by God's grace loosed, or by God's judgment not loosed, when infants die, they pass, on the one hand, by the merit of regeneration from evil to good, or on the other, by the merit of their origin from evil to evil. The catholic faith acknowledges this, and even some heretics, without any contradiction, agree to this. But in the height of wonder and astonishment I am unable to discover whence men, whose intelligence your letters show to be by no means contemptible, could entertain the opinion that any one should be judged not according to the merits that he had as long as he was in the body, but according to the merits which he would have had if he had lived longer in the body; and I should not dare to believe that there were such men, if I could venture to disbelieve you. But I hope that God will interpose, so that when they are admonished they may at once perceive, that if those sins which, as is said, would have been, can rightly be punished by God's judgment in those who are not baptized, they may also be rightly remitted by God's grace in those who are baptized. For whoever says that future sins can only be punished by God's judgment, but cannot be pardoned by God's mercy, ought to consider how great a wrong he is doing to God and His grace; as if future sin could be foreknown, and could not be foregone. And if this is absurd, it is the greater reason that help should be afforded to those who would be sinners if they lived longer, when they die in early life, by means of that laver wherein sins are washed away.

Chapter 25 [XIII.]—Possibly the Baptized Infants Would Have Repented If They Had Lived, and the Unbaptized Not.

But if, perchance, they say that sins are re-remitted to penitents, and that those who die in infancy are not baptized because they are foreknown as not such as would repent if they should live, while God has foreknown that those who are baptized and die in infancy would have repented if they had lived, let them observe and see that if it be so it is not in this case original sins which are punished in infants that die without baptism, but what would have been the sins of each one had he lived; and also in baptized infants, that it is not original sins that are washed away, but their own future sins if they should live, since they could not sin except in more mature age; but that some were foreseen as such as would repent, and others as such as would not repent, therefore some were baptized, and others departed from this life without baptism. If the Pelagians should dare to say this, by their denial of original sin they would thus be relieved of the necessity of seeking, on behalf of infants outside of the kingdom of God, for some place of I know not what happiness of their own; especially since they are convinced that they cannot have eternal life because they have not eaten the flesh nor drank the blood of Christ; and because in them who have no sin at all, baptism, which is given for the remission of sins, is falsified. For they would go on to say that there is no original sin, but that those who as infants are released are either baptized or not baptized according to their future merits if they should live, and that according to their future merits they either receive or do not receive the body and blood of Christ, without which they absolutely cannot have life; and are baptized for the true remission of sins although they derived no sins from Adam, because the sins are remitted unto them concerning which God foreknew that they would repent. Thus with the greatest ease they would plead and would win their cause, in which they deny that there is any original sin, and contend that the grace of God is only given according to our merits. But that the future merits of men, which merits will never come into existence are beyond all doubt no merits at all, it is certainly most easy to see: for this reason even the Pelagians were not able to say this; and much rather these ought not to say it. For it cannot be said with what pain I find that they who with us on catholic authority condemn the error of those heretics, have not seen this, which the Pelagians themselves have seen to be most false and absurd.

Chapter 26 [XIV]—Reference to Cyprian's Treatise "On the Mortality."

Cyprian wrote a work On the Mortality, known with approval to many and almost all who love ecclesiastical literature, wherein he says that death is not only not disadvantageous to believers, but that it is even found to be advantageous, because it withdraws men from the risks of sinning, and establishes them in a security of not sinning. But wherein is the advantage of this, if even future sins which have not been committed are punished? Yet he argues most copiously and well that the risks of sinning are not wanting in this life, and that they do not continue after this life is done; where also he adduces that testimony from the book of Wisdom: "He was taken away, lest wickedness should alter his understanding." And this was also adduced by me, though you said that those brethren of yours had rejected it on the ground of its not having been brought forward from a canonical book; as if, even setting aside the attestation of this book, the thing itself were not clear which I wished to be taught therefrom. For what Christian would dare to deny that the righteous man, if he should be prematurely laid hold of by death, will be in repose? Let who will, say this, and what man of sound faith will think that he can withstand it? Moreover, if he should say that the righteous man, if he should depart from his righteousness in which he has long lived, and should die in that impiety after having lived in it, I say not a year, but one day, will go hence into the punishment due to the wicked, his righteousness having no power in the future to avail him, —will any believer contradict this evident truth? Further, if we are asked whether, if he had died then at the time that he was righteous, he would have incurred punishment or repose, shall we hesitate to answer, repose? This is the whole reason why it is said, —whoever says it, — "He was taken away lest wickedness should alter his understanding." For it was said about the risks of this life, not with reference to the foreknowledge of God, who foreknew that which was to be, not that which was not to be—that is, that He would bestow on him an untimely death in order that he might be withdrawn from the uncertainty of temptations; not that he would sin, since he was not to remain in temptation. Because, concerning this life, we read in the book of Job, "Is not the life of man upon earth a temptation?" But why it should be granted to some to be taken away from the perils of this life while they are righteous, while others who are righteous until they fall from righteousness are kept in the same risks in a more lengthened life, —who has known the mind of the Lord? And yet it is permitted to be understood from this, that even those righteous people who maintain good and pious characters, even to the maturity of old age and to the last day of this life, must not glory in their own merits, but in the Lord, since He who took away the righteous man from the shortness of life, lest wickedness should alter his understanding, Himself guards the righteous man in any length of life, that wickedness may not alter his understanding. But why He should have kept the righteous man here to fall, when He might have withdrawn him before, —His judgments, although absolutely righteous, are yet unsearchable.

Chapter 27. —The Book of Wisdom Obtains in the Church the Authority of Canonical Scripture.

And since these things are so, the judgment of the book of Wisdom ought not to be repudiated, since for so long a course of years that book has deserved to be read in the Church of Christ from the station of the readers of the Church of Christ, and to be heard by all Christians, from bishops downwards, even to the lowest lay believers, penitents, and catechumens, with the veneration paid to divine authority. For assuredly, if, from those who have been before me in commenting on the divine Scriptures, I should bring forward a defense of this judgment, which we are now called upon to defend more carefully and copiously than usual against the new error of the Pelagians,—that is, that God's grace is not given according to our merits, and that it is given freely to whom it is given, because it is neither of him that wills, nor of him that runs, but of God that shows mercy; but that by righteous judgment it is not given to whom it is not given, because there is no unrighteousness with God;—if, therefore, I should put forth a defense of this opinion from catholic commentators on the divine oracles who have preceded us, assuredly these brethren for whose sake I am now discoursing would acquiesce, for this you have intimated in your letters. What need is there, then, for us to investigate the writings of those who, before this heresy sprang up, had no necessity to be conversant in a question so difficult of solution as this, which beyond a doubt they would have done if they had been compelled to answer such things? Whence it arose that they touched upon what they thought of God's grace briefly in some passages of their writings, and cursorily; but on those matters which they argued against the enemies of the Church, and in exhortations to every virtue by which to serve the living and true God for the purpose of attaining eternal life and true happiness, they dwelt at length. But the grace of God, what it could do, shows itself artlessly by its frequent mention in prayers; for what God commands to be done would not be asked for from God, unless it could be given by Him that it should be done.

Chapter 28. —Cyprian's Treatise "On the Mortality."

But if any wish to be instructed in the opinions of those who have handled the subject, it behooves them to prefer to all commentators the book of Wisdom, where it is read, "He was taken away, that wickedness should not alter his understanding;" because illustrious commentators, even in the times nearest to the apostles, preferred it to themselves, seeing that when they made use of it for a testimony they believed that they were making use of nothing but a divine testimony; and certainly it appears that the most blessed Cyprian, in order to commend the advantage of an earlier death, contended that those who end this life, wherein sin is possible, are taken away from the risks of sins. In the same treatise, among other things, he says, "Why, when you are about to be with Christ, and are secure of the divine promise, do you not embrace being called to Christ, and rejoice that you are free from the devil?" And in another place he says, "Boys escape the peril of their unstable age." And again, in another place, he says, "Why do we not hasten and run, that we may see our country, that we may hail our relatives? A great number of those who are dear to us are expecting us there, —a dense and abundant crowd of parents, brethren, sons, are longing for us; already secure of their own safety, but still anxious about our salvation." By these and such like sentiments, that teacher sufficiently and plainly testifies, in the clearest light of the catholic faith, that perils of sin and trials are to be feared even until the putting off of this body, but that afterwards no one shall suffer any such things. And even if he did not testify thus, when could any manner of Christian be in doubt on this matter? How, then, should it not have been of advantage to a man who has lapsed, and who finishes his life wretchedly in that same state of lapse, and passes into the punishment due to such as he, —how, I say, should it not have been of the greatest and highest advantage to such a one to be snatched by death from this sphere of temptations before his fall?

Chapter 29. —God's Dealing Does Not Depend Upon Any Contingent Merits of Men.

And thus, unless we indulge in reckless disputation, the entire question is concluded concerning him who is taken away lest wickedness should alter his understanding. And the book of Wisdom, which for such a series of years has deserved to be read in Christ's Church, and in which this is read, ought not to suffer injustice because it withstands those who are mistaken on behalf of men's merit, so as to come in opposition to the most manifest grace of God: and this grace chiefly appears in infants, and while some of these baptized, and some not baptized, come to the end of this life, they sufficiently point to God's mercy and His judgment,—His mercy, indeed, gratuitous, His judgment, of debt. For if men should be judged according to the merits of their life, which merits they have been prevented by death from actually having, but would have had if they had lived, it would be of no advantage to him who is taken away lest wickedness should alter his understanding; it would be of no advantage to those who die in a state of lapse if they should die before. And this no Christian will venture to say. Wherefore our brethren, who with us on behalf of the catholic faith assail the pest of the Pelagian error, ought not to such an extent to favor the Pelagian opinion, wherein they conceive that God's grace is given according to our merits, as to endeavor (which they cannot dare) to invalidate a true sentiment, plainly and from ancient times Christian,—"He was taken away, lest wickedness should alter his understanding;" and to build up that which we should think, I do not say, no one would believe, but no one would dream,—to wit, that any deceased person would be judged according to those things which he would have done if he had lived for a more lengthened period. Surely thus what we say manifests itself clearly to be incontestable, —that the grace of God is not given according to our merits; so that ingenious men who contradict this truth are constrained to say things which must be rejected from the ears and from the thoughts of all men.

Chapter 30 [XV.]—The Most Illustrious Instance of Predestination is Christ Jesus.

Moreover, the most illustrious Light of predestination and grace is the Savior Himself, —the Mediator Himself between God and men, the man Christ Jesus. And, pray, by what preceding merits of its own, whether of works or of faith, did the human nature which is in Him procure for itself that it should be this? Let this have an answer, I beg. That man, whence did He deserve this—to be assumed by the Word co-eternal with the Father into unity of person, and be the only-begotten Son of God? Was it because any kind of goodness in Him preceded? What did He do before? What did He believe? What did He ask, that He should attain to this unspeakable excellence? Was it not by the act and the assumption of the Word that that man, from the time He began to be, began to be the only Son of God? Did not that woman, full of grace, conceive the only Son of God? Was He not born the only Son of God, of the Holy Spirit and the Virgin Mary, —not of the lust of the flesh, but by God's peculiar gift? Was it to be feared that as age matured this man, He would sin of free will? Or was the will in Him not free on that account? and was it not so much the freer in proportion to the greater impossibility of His becoming the servant of sin? Certainly, in Him human nature—that is to say, our nature—specially received all those especially admirable gifts, and any others that may most truly be said to be peculiar to Him, by virtue of no preceding merits of its own. Let a man here answer to God if he dares, and say, Why was it not I also? And if he should hear, "O man, who art thou that replies against God?" let him not at this point restrain himself, but increase his impudence and say, "How is it that I hear, Who art thou, O man? since I am what I hear, —that is, a man, and He of whom I speak is but the same? Why should not I also be what He is? For it is by grace that He is such and so great; why is grace different when nature is common? Assuredly, there is no respect of persons with God." I say, not what Christian man, but what madman will say this?

Chapter 31. —Christ Predestinated to Be the Son of God.

Therefore, in Him who is our Head let there appear to be the very fountain of grace, whence, according to the measure of every man, He diffuses Himself through all His members. It is by that grace that every man from the beginning of his faith becomes a Christian, by which grace that one man from His beginning became Christ. Of the same Spirit also the former is born again of which the latter was born. By the same Spirit is affected in us the remission of sins, by which Spirit it was affected that He should have no sin. God certainly foreknew that He would do these things. This, therefore, is that same predestination of the saints which most especially shone forth in the Saint of saints; and who is there of those who rightly understand the declarations of the truth that can deny this predestination? For we have learned that the Lord of glory Himself was predestinated in so far as the man was made the Son of God. The teacher of the Gentiles exclaims, in the beginning of his epistles, "Paul, a servant of Jesus Christ, called to be an apostle, separated unto the gospel of God (which He had promised afore by His prophets in the Holy Scriptures) concerning His Son, which was made of the seed of David according to the flesh, who was predestinated the Son of God in power, according to the Spirit of sanctification by the resurrection of the dead." Therefore Jesus was predestinated, so that He who was to be the Son of David according to the flesh should yet be in power the Son of God, according to the Spirit of sanctification, because He was born of the Holy Spirit and of the Virgin Mary. This is that ineffably accomplished sole taking up of man by God the Word, so that He might truly and properly be called at the same time the Son of God and the Son of man, —Son of man because of the man taken up, and the Son of God because of the God only-begotten who took Him up, so that a Trinity and not a Quaternity might be believed in. Such a transporting of human nature was predestinated, so great, so lofty, and so sublime that there was no exalting it more highly, —just as on our behalf that divinity had no possibility of more humbly putting itself off, than by the assumption of man's nature with the weakness of the flesh, even to the death of the cross. As, therefore, that one man was predestinated to be our Head, so we being many are predestinated to be His members. Here let human merits which have perished through Adam keep silence and let that grace of God reign which reigns through Jesus Christ our Lord, the only Son of God, the one Lord. Let whoever can find in our Head the merits which preceded that peculiar generation, seek in us His members for those merits which preceded our manifold regeneration. For that generation was not recompensed to Christ, but given; that He should be born, namely, of the Spirit and the Virgin, separate from all entanglement of sin. Thus, also our being born again of water and the Spirit is not recompensed to us for any merit, but freely given; and if faith has brought us to the laver of regeneration, we ought not therefore to suppose that we have first given anything, so that the regeneration of salvation should be recompensed to us again; because He made us to believe in Christ, who made for us a Christ on whom we believe. He makes in men the beginning and the completion of the faith in Jesus who made the man Jesus the beginner and finisher of faith; for thus, as you know, He is called in the epistle which is addressed to the Hebrews.

Chapter 32 [XVI.]—The Twofold Calling.

God indeed calls many predestinated children of His, to make them members of His only predestinated Son,—not with that calling with which they were called who would not come to the marriage, since with that calling were called also the Jews, to whom Christ crucified is an offence, and the Gentiles, to whom Christ crucified is foolishness; but with that calling He calls the predestinated which the apostle distinguished when he said that he preached Christ, the wisdom of God and the power of God, to them that were called, Jews as well as Greeks. For thus he says, "But unto them which are called," in order to show that there were some who were not called; knowing that there is a certain sure calling of those who are called according to God's purpose, whom He has foreknown and predestinated before to be conformed to the image of His Son. And it was this calling he meant when he said, "Not of works, but of Him that calleth; it was said unto her, That the elder shall serve the younger." Did he say, "Not of works, but of him that believeth"? Rather, he actually took this away from man, that he might give the whole to God. Therefore he said, "But of Him that calleth,"—not with any sort of calling whatever, but with that calling wherewith a man is made a believer.

Chapter 33. —It is in the Power of Evil Men to Sin; But to Do This or That by Means of that Wickedness is in God's Power Alone.

Moreover, it was this that he had in view when he said, "The gifts and calling of God are without repentance." And in that saying also consider for a little what was its purport. For when he had said, "For I would not, brethren, that ye should be ignorant of this mystery, that ye may not be wise in yourselves, that blindness in part is happened to Israel, until the fulness of the Gentiles be come in, and so all Israel should be saved; as it is written, There shall come out of Sion one who shall deliver, and turn away impiety from Jacob: and this is the covenant to them from me, when I shall take away their sins;" he immediately added, what is to be very carefully understood, "As concerning the gospel, indeed, they are enemies for your sakes: but as concerning the election, they are beloved for their fathers' sakes." What is the meaning of, "as concerning the gospel, indeed, they are enemies for your sake," but that their enmity wherewith they put Christ to death was, without doubt, as we see, an advantage to the gospel? And he shows that this came about by God's ordering, who knew how to make a good use even of evil things; not that the vessels of wrath might be of advantage to Him, but that by His own good use of them they might be of advantage to the vessels of mercy. For what could be said more plainly than what is actually said, "As concerning the gospel, indeed, they are enemies for your sakes"? It is, therefore, in the power of the wicked to sin; but that in sinning they should do this or that by that wickedness is not in their power, but in God's, who divides the darkness and regulates it; so that hence even what they do contrary to God's will is not fulfilled except it be God's will. We read in the Acts of the Apostles that when the apostles had been sent away by the Jews, and had come to their own friends, and shown them what great things the priests and elders said to them, they all with one consent lifted up their voices to the Lord and said, "Lord, thou art God, which hast made heaven, and earth, and the sea, and all things that are therein; who, by the mouth of our father David, thy holy servant, hast said, Why did the heathen rage, and the peoples imagine vain things? The kings of the earth stood up, and the princes were gathered together against the Lord, and against His Christ. For in truth, there have assembled together in this city against Thy holy child Jesus, whom Thou hast anointed, Herod and Pilate, and the people of Israel, to do whatever Thy hand and counsel predestinated to be done." See what is said: "As concerning the gospel, indeed, they are enemies for your sakes." Because God's hand and counsel predestinated such things to be done by the hostile Jews as were necessary for the gospel, for our sakes. But what is it that follows? "But as concerning the election, they are beloved for their fathers' sakes." For are those enemies who perished in their enmity and those of the same people who still perish in their opposition to Christ, —are those chosen and beloved? Away with the thought! Who is so utterly foolish as to say this? But both expressions, although contrary to one another—that is, "enemies" and "beloved"—are appropriate, though not to the same men, yet to the same Jewish people, and to the same carnal seed of lsrael, of whom some belonged to the falling away, and some to the blessing of Israel himself. For the apostle previously explained this meaning more clearly when he said, "That which lsrael wrought for, he hath not obtained; but the election hath obtained it, and the rest were blinded?" Yet in both cases it was the very same Israel. Where, therefore, we hear, "Israel hath not obtained," or, "The rest were blinded," there are to be understood the enemies for our sakes; but where we hear, "that the election hath obtained it," there are to be understood the beloved for their father's sakes, to which fathers those things were assuredly promised; because "the promises were made to Abraham and his seed," whence also in that olive-tree is grafted the wild olive-tree of the Gentiles. Now subsequently we certainly ought to fall in with the election, of which he says that it is according to grace, not according to debt, because "there was made a remnant by the election of grace" This election obtained it, the rest being blinded. As concerning this election, the Israelites were beloved for the sake of their fathers. For they were not called with that calling of which it is said, "Many are called," but with that whereby the chosen are called. Whence also after he had said, "But as concerning the election, they are beloved for the fathers' sakes," he went on to add those words whence this discussion arose: "For the gifts and calling of God are without repentance,"—that is, they are firmly established without change. Those who belong to this calling are all teachable by God; nor can any of them say, "I believed in order to being thus called," because the mercy of God anticipated him, because he was so called in order that he might believe. For all who are teachable of God come to the Son because they have heard and learned from the Father through the Son, who most clearly says, "Everyone who has heard of the Father, and has learned, cometh unto me." But of such as these none perishes, because "of all that the Father hath given Him, He will lose none." Whoever, therefore, is of these does not perish at all; nor was any who perishes ever of these. For which reason it is said, "They went out from among us, but they were not of us; for if they had been of us, they would certainly have continued with us."

Chapter 34 [XVII.]—The Special Calling of the Elect is Not Because They Have Believed, But in Order that They May Believe.

Let us, then, understand the calling whereby they become elected, —not those who are elected because they have believed, but who are elected that they may believe. For the Lord Himself also sufficiently explains this calling when He says, "Ye have not chosen me, but I have chosen you." For if they had been elected because they had believed, they themselves would certainly have first chosen Him by believing in Him, so that they should deserve to be elected. But He takes away this supposition altogether when He says, "Ye have not chosen me, but I have chosen you." And yet they themselves, beyond a doubt, chose Him when they believed on Him. Whence it is not for any other reason that He says, "Ye have not chosen me, but I have chosen you," than because they did not choose Him that He should choose them, but He chose them that they might choose Him; because His mercy preceded them according to grace, not according to debt. Therefore, He chose them out of the world while He was wearing flesh, but as those who were already chosen in Himself before the foundation of the world. This is the changeless truth concerning predestination and grace. For what is it that the apostle says, "As He hath chosen us in Himself before the foundation of the world"? And assuredly, if this were said because God foreknew that they would believe, not because He Himself would make them believers, the Son is speaking against such a foreknowledge as that when He says, "Ye have not chosen me, but I have chosen you;" when God should rather have foreknown this very thing, that they themselves would have chosen Him, so that they might deserve to be chosen by Him. Therefore, they were elected before the foundation of the world with that predestination in which God foreknew what He Himself would do; but they were elected out of the world with that calling whereby God fulfilled that which He predestinated. For whom He predestinated, them He also called, with that calling, to wit, which is according to the purpose. Not others, therefore, but those whom He predestinated, them He also called; nor others, but those whom He so called, them He also justified; nor others, but those whom He predestinated, called, and justified, them He also glorified; assuredly to that end which has no end.

Therefore God elected believers; but He chose them that they might be so, not because they were already so. The Apostle James says: "Has not God chosen the poor in this world, rich in faith, and heirs of the kingdom which God hath promised to them that love Him?" By choosing them, therefore; He makes them rich in faith, as He makes them heirs of the kingdom; because He is rightly said to choose that in them, in order to make which in them He chose them. I ask, who can hear the Lord saying, "Ye have not chosen me, but I have chosen you," and can dare to say that men believe in order to be elected, when they are rather elected to believe; lest against the judgment of truth they be found to have first chosen Christ to whom Christ says, "Ye have not chosen me, but I have chosen you"?

Chapter 35 [XVIII.]—Election is for the Purpose of Holiness.

Who can hear the apostle saying, "Blessed be the God and Father of our Lord Jesus Christ, who hath blessed us in all spiritual blessing in the heavens in Christ; as He has chosen us in Him before the foundation of the world, that we should be holy and without spot in His sight; in love predestinating us to the adoption of children by Jesus Christ to Himself according to the good pleasure of His will, wherein He hath shown us favor in His beloved Son; in whom we have redemption through His blood, the remission of sins according to the riches of His grace, which hath abounded to us in all wisdom and prudence; that He might show to us the mystery of His will according to His good pleasure, which He hath purposed in Himself, in the dispensation of the fulness of times, to restore all things in Christ, which are in heaven, and in the earth, in Him: in whom also we have obtained a share, being predestinated according to the purpose; who worketh all things according to the counsel of His will, that we should be to the praise of his glory;"—who, I say, can hear these words with attention and intelligence, and can venture to have any doubt concerning a truth so clear as this which we are defending? God chose Christ's members in Him before the foundation of the world; and how should He choose those who as yet did not exist, except by predestinating them? Therefore He chose us by predestinating us. Would he choose the unholy and the unclean? Now if the question be proposed, whether He would choose such, or rather the holy and unstained, who can ask which of these he may answer, and not give his opinion at once in favor of the holy and pure?

Chapter 36. —God Chose the Righteous; Not Those Whom He Foresaw as Being of Themselves, But Those Whom He Predestinated for the Purpose of Making So.

"Therefore," says the Pelagian, "He foreknew who would be holy and immaculate by the choice of free will, and on that account elected them before the foundation of the world in that same foreknowledge of His in which He foreknew that they would be such. Therefore He elected them," says he, "before they existed, predestinating them to be children whom He foreknew to be holy and immaculate. Certainly He did not make them so; nor did He foresee that He would make them so, but that they would be so." Let us, then, investigate the words of the apostle and see whether He chose us before the foundation of the world because we were going to be holy and immaculate, or in order that we might be so. "Blessed," says he, "be the God and Father of our Lord Jesus Christ, who hath blessed us in all spiritual blessing in the heavens in Christ; even as He hath chosen us in Himself before the foundation of the world, that we should be holy and unspotted." Not, then, because we were to be so, but that we might be so. Assuredly it is certain, —assuredly it is manifest. Certainly, we were to be such because He has chosen us, predestinating us to be such by His grace. Therefore "He blessed us with spiritual blessing in the heavens in Christ Jesus, even as He chose us in Him before the foundation of the world, that we should be holy and immaculate in His sight, in order that we might not in so great a benefit of grace glory concerning the good pleasure of our will. "In which," says he, "He hath shown us favor in His beloved Son,"—in which, certainly, His own will, He hath shown us favor. Thus, it is said, He hath shown us grace by grace, even as it is said, He has made us righteous by righteousness. "In whom," he says, "we have redemption through His blood, the forgiveness of sins, according to the riches of His grace, which has abounded to us in all wisdom and prudence; that he might show to us the mystery of His will, according to His good pleasure." In this mystery of His will, He placed the riches of His grace, according to His good pleasure, not according to ours, which could not possibly be good unless He Himself, according to His own good pleasure, should aid it to become so. But when he had said, "According to His good pleasure," he added, "which He purposed in Him," that is, in His beloved Son, "in the dispensation of the fulness of times to restore all things in Christ, which are in heaven, and which are in earth, in Him: in whom also we too have obtained a lot, being predestinated according to His purpose who worketh all things according to the counsel of His will; that we should be to the praise of His glory."

Chapter 37. —We Were Elected and Predestinated, Not Because We Were Going to Be Holy, But in Order that We Might Be So.

It would be too tedious to argue about the several points. But you see without doubt, you see with what evidence of apostolic declaration this grace is defended, in opposition to which human merits are set up, as if man should first give something for it to be recompensed to him again. Therefore, God chose us in Christ before the foundation of the world, predestinating us to the adoption of children, not because we were going to be of ourselves holy and immaculate, but He chose and predestinated us that we might be so. Moreover, He did this according to the good pleasure of His will, so that nobody might glory concerning his own will, but about God's will towards himself. He did this according to the riches of His grace, according to His good-will, which He purposed in His beloved Son; in whom we have obtained a share, being predestinated according to the purpose, not ours, but His, who worketh all things to such an extent as that He worketh in us to will also. Moreover, He worketh according to the counsel of His will, that we may be to the praise of His glory. For this reason, it is that we cry that no one should glory in man, and, thus, not in himself; but whoever glories let him glory in the Lord, that he may be for the praise of His glory. Because He Himself worketh according to His purpose that we may be to the praise of His glory, and, of course, holy and immaculate, for which purpose He called us, predestinating us before the foundation of the world. Out of this, His purpose, is that special calling of the elect for whom He co-worketh with all things for good, because they are called according to His purpose, and "the gifts and calling of God are without repentance."

Chapter 38 [XIX.]—What is the View of the Pelagians, and What of the Semi-Pelagians, Concerning Predestination.

But these brethren of ours, about whom and on whose behalf, we are now discoursing, say, perhaps, that the Pelagians are refuted by this apostolical testimony in which it is said that we are chosen in Christ and predestinated before the foundation of the world, in order that we should be holy and immaculate in His sight in love. For they think that "having received God's commands we are of ourselves by the choice of our free will made holy and immaculate in His sight in love; and since God foresaw that this would be the case," they say, "He therefore chose and predestinated us in Christ before the foundation of the world." Although the apostle says that it was not because He foreknew that we should be such, but in order that we might be such by the same election of His grace, by which He showed us favor in His beloved Son. When, therefore, He predestinated us, He foreknew His own work by which He makes us holy and immaculate. Whence the Pelagian error is rightly refuted by this testimony. "But we say," say they, "that God did not foreknow anything as ours except that faith by which we begin to believe, and that He chose and predestinated us before the foundation of the world, in order that we might be holy and immaculate by His grace and by His work." But let them also hear in this testimony the words where he says, "We have obtained a lot, being predestinated according to His purpose who worketh all things." He, therefore, worketh the beginning of our belief who worketh all things; because faith itself does not precede that calling of which it is said: "For the gifts and calling of God are without repentance;" and of which it is said: "Not of works, but of Him that calleth" (although He might have said, "of Him that believeth"); and the election which the Lord signified when He said: "Ye have not chosen me, but I have chosen you." For He chose us, not because we believed, but that we might believe, lest we should be said first to have chosen Him, and so His word be false (which be it far from us to think possible), "Ye have not chosen me, but I have chosen you." Neither are we called because we believed, but that we may believe; and by that calling which is without repentance it is affected and carried through that we should believe. But all the many things which we have said concerning this matter need not to be repeated.

Chapter 39—The Beginning of Faith is God's Gift.

Finally, also, in what follows this testimony, the apostle gives thanks to God on behalf of those who have believed; —not, certainly, because the gospel has been declared to them, but because they have believed. For he says, "In whom also after ye had heard the word of truth, the gospel of your salvation; in whom also, after that ye believed, ye were sealed with the Holy Spirit of promise, which is the pledge of our inheritance, to the redemption of the purchased possession unto the praise of His glory. Wherefore I also, after I had heard of your faith in Christ Jesus and with reference to all the saints, cease not to give thanks for you." Their faith was new and recent on the preaching of the gospel to them, which faith when he hears of, the apostle gives thanks to God on their behalf. If he were to give thanks to man for that which he might either think or know that man had not given, it would be called a flattery or a mockery, rather than a giving of thanks. "Do not err, for God is not mocked;" for His gift is also the beginning of faith, unless the apostolic giving of thanks be rightly judged to be either mistaken or fallacious. What then? Does that not appear as the beginning of the faith of the Thessalonians, for which, nevertheless, the same apostle gives thanks to God when he says, "For this cause also we thank God without ceasing, because when ye had received from us the word of the hearing of God, ye received it not as the word of men, but as it is in truth the word of God, which effectually worketh in you and which ye believed"? What is that for which he here gives thanks to God? Assuredly it is a vain and idle thing if He to whom he gives thanks did not Himself do the thing. But, since this is not a vain and idle thing, certainly God, to whom he gave thanks concerning this work, Himself did it; that when they had received the word of the hearing of God, they received it not as the word of men, but as it is in truth the word of God. God, therefore, worketh in the hearts of men with that calling according to His purpose, of which we have spoken a great deal, that they should not hear the gospel in vain, but when they heard it, should be converted and believe, receiving it not as the word of men, but as it is in truth the word of God.

Chapter 40 [XX.]—Apostolic Testimony to the Beginning of Faith Being God's Gift.

Moreover, we are admonished that the beginning of men's faith is God's gift, since the apostle signifies this when, in the Epistle to the Colossians, he says, "Continue in prayer, and watch in the same in giving of thanks. Withal praying also for us that God would open unto us the door of His word, to speak the mystery of Christ, for which also I am in bonds, that I may so make it manifest as I ought to speak." How is the door of His word opened, except when the sense of the hearer is opened so that he may believe, and, having made a beginning of faith, may admit those things which are declared and reasoned, for the purpose of building up wholesome doctrine, lest, by a heart closed through unbelief, he rejects and repel those things which are spoken? Whence, also, he says to the Corinthians: "But I will tarry at Ephesus until Pentecost. For a great and evident door is opened unto me, and there are many adversaries." What else can be understood here, save that, when the gospel had been first of all preached there by him, many had believed, and there had appeared many adversaries of the same faith, in accordance with that saying of the Lord, "No one cometh unto me, unless it were given him of my Father;" and, "To you it is given to know the mysteries of the kingdom of heaven, but to them it is not given"? Therefore, there is an open door in those to whom it is given, but there are many adversaries among those to whom it is not given.

Chapter 41. —Further Apostolic Testimonies.

And again, the same apostle says to the same people, in his second Epistle: "When I had come to Troas for the gospel of Christ, and a door had been opened unto me in the Lord, I had no rest in my spirit, because I found not Titus, my brother: but, making my farewell to them, I went away into Macedonia." To whom did he bid farewell but to those who had believed, —to wit, in whose hearts the door was opened for his preaching of the gospel? But attend to what he adds, saying, "Now thanks be unto God, who always causes us to triumph in Christ, and makes manifest the savor of His knowledge by us in every place: because we are unto God a sweet savor of Christ in them who are saved, and in them who perish: to some, indeed, we are the savor of death unto death, but to some the savor of life unto life." See concerning what this most zealous soldier and invincible defender of grace gives thanks. See concerning what he gives thanks, —that the apostles are a sweet savor of Christ unto God, both in those who are saved by His grace, and in those who perish by His judgment. But in order that those who little understand these things may be less enraged, he himself gives a warning when he adds the words: "And who is sufficient for these things?" But let us return to the opening of the door by which the apostle signified the beginning of faith in his hearers. For what is the meaning of, "Withal praying also for us that God would open unto us a door of the word," unless it is a most manifest demonstration that even the very beginning of faith is the gift of God? For it would not be sought for from Him in prayer, unless it were believed to be given by Him. This gift of heavenly grace had descended to that seller of purple for whom, as Scripture says in the Acts of the Apostles, "The Lord opened her heart, and she gave heed unto the things which were said by Paul;" for she was so called that she might believe. Because God does what He will in the hearts of men, either by assistance or by judgment; so that, even through their means, may be fulfilled what His hand and counsel have predestinated to be done.

Chapter 42. —Old Testament Testimonies.

Therefore also it is in vain that objectors have alleged, that what we have proved by Scripture testimony from the books of Kings and Chronicles is not pertinent to the subject of which we are discoursing: such, for instance, as that when God wills that to be done which ought only to be done by the willing men, their hearts are inclined to will this,—inclined, that is to say, by His power, who, in a marvelous and ineffable manner, worketh in us also to will. What else is this than to say nothing, and yet to contradict? Unless perchance, they have given some reason to you for the view that they have taken, which reason you have preferred to say nothing about in your letters. But what that reason can be I do not know. Whether, possibly, since we have shown that God has so acted on the hearts of men, and has induced the wills of those whom He pleased to this point, that Saul or David should be established as king, —do they not think that these instances are appropriate to this subject, because to reign in this world temporally is not the same thing as to reign eternally with God? And so do they suppose that God inclines the wills of those whom He pleases to the attainment of earthly kingdoms, but does not incline them to the attainment of a heavenly kingdom? But I think that it was in reference to the kingdom of heaven, and not to an earthly kingdom, that it was said, "Incline my heart unto Thy testimonies;" or, "The steps of a man are ordered by the Lord, and He will will His way;" or, "The will is prepared by the Lord;" or, "Let our Lord be with us as with our fathers; let Him not forsake us, nor turn Himself away from us; let Him incline our hearts unto Him, that we may walk in all His ways;" or, "I will give them a heart to know me, and ears that hear;" or, "I will give them another heart, and a new spirit will I give them." Let them also hear this, "I will give my Spirit within you, and I will cause you to walk in my righteousness; and ye shall observe my judgments, and do them." Let them hear, "Man's goings are directed by the Lord, and how can a man understand His ways?" Let them hear, "Every man seems right to himself, but the Lord directs the hearts." Let them hear, "As many as were ordained to eternal life believed." Let them hear these passages, and whatever others of the kind I have not mentioned in which God is declared to prepare and to convert men's wills, even for the kingdom of heaven and for eternal life. And consider what sort of a thing it is to believe that God worketh men's wills for the foundation of earthly kingdoms, but that men work their own wills for the attainment of the kingdom of heaven.

Chapter 43 [XXI.]—Conclusion.

I have said a great deal, and, perchance, I could long ago have persuaded you what I wished, and am still speaking this to such intelligent minds as if they were obtuse, to whom even what is too much is not enough. But let them pardon me, for a new question has compelled me to this. Because, although in my former little treatises I had proved by sufficiently appropriate proofs that faith also was the gift of God, there was found this ground of contradiction, viz., that those testimonies were good for this purpose, to show that the increase of faith was God's gift, but that the beginning of faith, whereby a man first of all believes in Christ, is of the man himself, and is not the gift of God,—but that God requires this, so that when it has preceded, other gifts may follow, as it were on the ground of this merit, and these are the gifts of God; and that none of them is given freely, although in them God's grace is declared, which is not grace except as being gratuitous. And you see how absurd all this is. Wherefore I determined, as far as I could, to set forth that this very beginning also is God's gift. And if I have done this at a greater length than perhaps those on whose account I did it might wish, I am prepared to be reproached for it by them, so long as they nevertheless confess that, although at greater length than they wished, although with the disgust and weariness of those that understand, I have done what I have done: that is, I have taught that even the beginning of faith, as continence, patience, righteousness, piety, and the rest, concerning which there is no dispute with them, is God's gift. Let this, therefore, be the end of this treatise, lest too great length in this one may give offence.

www.ingramcontent.com/pod-product-compliance
Ingram Content Group UK Ltd.
Pitfield, Milton Keynes, MK11 3LW, UK
UKHW020136250726
13967UKWH00002B/686